DEVRET CLARKE
Homosexuality
is a Mental Illness

HOMOSEXUALITY
IS A MENTAL ILLNESS

WRITTEN BY:

DEVRET CLARKE

Copyright © 2022 Devret Clarke

All rights reserved

ISBN: 9798848678765
Imprint: Independently published

~ Peace and Blessings ~

"Homosexuality is a Mental Illness". For those who think that is not, prove me wrong? If nature teaches us, why do the opposite? How can gays multiply? Why does sickness come once they defile themselves? In this book, I speak the truth on homosexuality, and how people that are gay/lesbian, better repent before it is too late.

Mental illness is a state of the mind that is playing tricks on the people. Those that claim to be homosexual, are in fact facing rebellious ways, and goes against nature for their own pleasure of sin.

For all those that claim to be homosexual, turn from the dark side, and turn to the light, for the light is truth. Time is at hand as this world is passing away. Do not fall for the agenda of the government, for it is to trap you, and to destroy your existence. Another trick by Satan to world depopulation, and to rob souls of eternal life. The Most High came with water before, now with flames. REPENT OR DIE!!!

Don't hate me for telling the truth, hate yourself for not accepting the truth.

— Devret Clarke -
website:www.devretclarke.ca

CHAPTERS
HOMOSEXUALITY IS A MENTAL ILLNESS

CHAPTER
1

GAY!
NOT BY NATURE,
BUT BY CHOICE
(THE BEGINGING OF MENTAL ILLNESS)

Being gay, is not something that you are born with, but something that you decide to do, and maybe even geared to do, by your parents. Still, it is a choice, and not by nature. A lot of times confusion will make a lot of people confused, and lack understanding, due to sin, and lust of the flesh, as well as, personal desires. Let me kick this off by telling you why being gay is not going to ever be by nature, and is a mental illness.

As we as Humans are created, we are not born confused. If you are born with a penis, you are a man, and if you are born with a vagina, you are a woman. There is no confusion, nor debate. Nature knows what it needs to survive, and by survival, we are intended to do what it takes to be the ultimate species upon the land, as well as, carry on life, for life is what is necessary for the world to be the world itself, and that is life within the world. Life would never exist if we were all by nature gay. How could we reproduce? There is no documented proof that homosexuals can reproduce without any form of scientific procedures. Sure, there is lab created babies that are not considered human, and are nothing but rat tested subjects. They are considered "test-tube babies". By nature, it takes a male, and a female. Let us go back to the beginning of time, and see how the Most High created man, and woman.

SCRIPTURE
Genesis 1:26-27
King James Version

26 And God said, Let us make man in our image, after our likeness: and let them have dominion over the fish of the sea, and over the fowl of the air, and over the cattle, and over all the earth, and over every creeping thing that creepeth upon the earth.

27 So God created man in his own image, in the image of God created he him; male and female created he them.

SCRIPTURE
Genesis 2:20-24
King James Version

20 And Adam gave names to all cattle, and to the fowl of the air, and to every beast of the field; but for Adam there was not found an help meet for him.

21 And the LORD God caused a deep sleep to fall upon Adam, and he slept: and he took one of his ribs, and closed up the flesh instead thereof;

22 **And the rib, which the LORD God had taken from man, made he a woman, and brought her unto the man.**

23 And Adam said, This is now bone of my bones, and flesh of my flesh: she shall be called **Woman**, because she was taken out of Man.

24 **Therefore shall a man leave his father and his mother, and shall cleave unto his wife: and they shall be one flesh.**

Now, as you can see, The Most High made man first upon the land. After making man, he made woman, being called so, by opening a womb within Adam, and taking the rib to make a woman. As the woman first came from man, and so, we now know that the Most High intended for HIS children to be male, and female, and to mate therein, to reproduce life, and continue to live. At no time in the Holy Scripture did this change. It took one male, and one female to create a child together. Even as they became one flesh.

S C R I P T U R E
Mark-10-6-9
King James Version

6 But from the beginning of the creation God made them male and female.

7 For this cause shall a man leave his father and mother, and cleave to his wife;

8 And they twain shall be one flesh: so then they are no more twain, but one flesh.

9 **What therefore God hath joined together, let not man put asunder.**

My question for all those homosexuals that still disagree is, how come the Most High didn't make Adam and Steve? How come HE didn't make Eve first? How come he made sure to make the opposite sex, and not the same sex? Okay, maybe you do not believe in the Most High, so lets wait for an answer from science. Can science debunk YAH (GOD)? Has science ever debunked the Most High? I got got another scripture for you whether you like it or not.

S C R I P T U R E
Job 38:4-13
King James Version

4 Where wast thou when I laid the foundations of the earth? declare, if thou hast understanding.

5 Who hath laid the measures thereof, if thou knowest? or who hath stretched the line upon it?

6 Whereupon are the foundations thereof fastened? or who laid the corner stone thereof;

7 When the morning stars sang together, and all the sons of God shouted for joy?

8 Or who shut up the sea with doors, when it brake forth, as if it had issued out of the womb?

9 When I made the cloud the garment thereof, and thick darkness a swaddlingband for it,

10 And brake up for it my decreed place, and set bars and doors,

11 And said, Hitherto shalt thou come, but no further: and here shall thy proud waves be stayed?

12 Hast thou commanded the morning since thy days; and caused the dayspring to know his place;

13 That it might take hold of the ends of the earth,
   that the wicked might be shaken out of it?

Truth to the matter is, we can never take away from YAH (GOD), nor can anyone debunk Creation from above. I have yet to hear a response, and will never hear it. They can say that there is a "BIG BANG" which is nothing but a false theory, stating that automatically the earth was formed, and how man came from monkeys and apes, yet there is still monkeys and apes walking this earth. Scientist can say we evolved from all sorts of other species, however, there is no proof of it, and if we evolved from any other species, those species should never exist today beneath us, (especially apes, and monkey's), but be apart of us, and even alongside us. That again will never happen. We are not from aliens, and we are not from any other creature. I will give you the scripture one more time.

SCRIPTURE
Genesis 1:27
King James Version

27 So God created man in his own image, in the image of God created he him; male and female

created he them.

To avoid any more confusion, we all look like the Most High, who is Alpha, and Omega. We can go deep into why the Most High is YAH (GOD) alone, but we need to skip the long route, knowing prophet is already being fulfilled, and displayed before our faces, if you can't see such things, you are too far gone anyways, and I am not going to spoon feed you things that you should already know. Now, going back to nature. I look at all the animals, all the sea creatures, all the birds/fowls of the air, and all the beast of the land, and even the creeping things, such as bugs/insects. All of which have male and female organs. Each of which know right to go with the opposite sex. Each of which that have understanding on how to re-creature/reproduce. Why? Because it works. That is the most basic, and factual explanation that I can give you. Now, as nature knows best, what confusion does Human kind have that they lack understanding in this area? It all goes back to science, and man being lovers of selves, while burning in lust for one another. Going even further, females mating with angels, create monsters. Seems that they are never satisfied.

SCRIPTURE
Romans 1:24-32
King James Version

24 Wherefore God also gave them up to uncleanness through the lusts of their own hearts, to dishonour their own bodies between themselves:

25 Who changed the truth of God into a lie, and worshipped and served the creature more than the Creator, who is blessed for ever. Amen.

26 For this cause God gave them up unto vile affections: for even their women did change the natural use into that which is against nature:

27 And likewise also the men, leaving the natural use of the woman, burned in their lust one toward another; men with men working that which is unseemly, and receiving in themselves that recompence of their error which was meet.

28 And even as they did not like to retain God in their knowledge, **God gave them over to a reprobate mind, to do those things which are not convenient;**

29 Being filled with all unrighteousness,

fornication, wickedness, covetousness, maliciousness; full of envy, murder, debate, deceit, malignity; whisperers,

30 Backbiters, haters of God, despiteful, proud, boasters, inventors of evil things, disobedient to parents,

31 Without understanding, covenantbreakers, without natural affection, implacable, unmerciful:

32 Who knowing the judgment of God, that they which commit such things are worthy of death, not only do the same, but have pleasure in them that do them.

"Men, leaving the natural use of the woman", is everything that went wrong. We all know that the wickedness of man is what made this world become filthy as it is today. The sin, the lust of the flesh, the materialistic things, and the polluted minds that all sum up the reasoning of errors. I can't forget those men and women that can't be content/satisfied. The loneliness of men has become so bad that they not only lusted after one another, but after all other species, including, trees, animals, and anything that they could claim as their "lover".

Sick and twisted they are. But who made them do such things? Is it nature, or self? When I say "nature", that includes YAH (GOD). Again, you need to go back and read the scripture (**Genesis** 2:24 KJV). We all know that man made their own choices, due to the Most High allowing them to do as thou wilt. They want to be gay, go ahead and be gay, but dot blame the Most High when you become sick with disease. See verse 28 of **Romans 1.** Knowing those that are filthy are corrupt minded, and evil. Women likewise, for the woman has also had relations with the trees, animals, and all sorts of materials, that they left the nature use of men for, which is disgusting.

SCRIPTURE
Job 38:4-13
King James Version

4 Where wast thou when I laid the foundations of the earth? declare, if thou hast understanding.

5 Who hath laid the measures thereof, if thou knowest? or who hath stretched the line upon it?

6 Whereupon are the foundations thereof fastened?
or who laid the corner stone thereof;

7 When the morning stars sang together, and all
the sons of God shouted for joy?

8 Or who shut up the sea with doors, when it brake
forth, as if it had issued out of the womb?

9 When I made the cloud the garment thereof, and
thick darkness a swaddlingband for it,

10 And brake up for it my decreed place, and set
bars and doors,

11 And said, Hitherto shalt thou come, but no
further: and here shall thy proud waves be stayed?

12 Hast thou commanded the morning since thy
days; and caused the dayspring to know his place;

13 That it might take hold of the ends of the earth,
that the wicked might be shaken out of it?

I want everyone that is a homosexual to give
me proof that reproduction can happen with
man/women and any other form of beast, fowl
of the air, sea creature, or insect. Truth is, if

they do such things, they create abominations that turn out very corrupt, deformed, and unnatural.

S C R I P T U R E
Genesis 6:1-13
King James Version

1 And it came to pass, when men began to multiply on the face of the earth, and daughters were born unto them,

2 That the sons of God saw the daughters of men that they were fair; and they took them wives of all which they chose.

3 And the Lord said, My spirit shall not always strive with man, for that he also is flesh: yet his days shall be an hundred and twenty years.

4 There were giants in the earth in those days; and also after that, when the sons of God came in unto the daughters of men, and they bare children to them, the same became mighty men which were of old, men of renown.

5 And God saw that the wickedness of man was great in the earth, and that every imagination of the thoughts of his heart was only evil continually.

6 And it repented the Lord that he had made man
on the earth, and it grieved him at his heart.

7 And the Lord said, I will destroy man whom I
have created from the face of the earth; both man,
and beast, and the creeping thing, and the fowls of
the air; for it repenteth me that I have made them.

8 But Noah found grace in the eyes of the Lord.

9 These are the generations of Noah: Noah was a
just man and perfect in his generations, and Noah
walked with God.

10 And Noah begat three sons, Shem, Ham, and
Japheth.

11 The earth also was corrupt before God, and the
earth was filled with violence.

12 And God looked upon the earth, and, behold, it
was corrupt; for all flesh had corrupted his way
upon the earth.

13 And God said unto Noah, The end of all flesh is
come before me; for the earth is filled with
violence through them; and, behold, I will destroy
them with the earth.

SCRIPTURE
Leviticus 18:22
King James Version

22 Thou shalt not lie with mankind, as with womankind: it is abomination.

SCRIPTURE
Leviticus 20:13
King James Version

13 If a man also lie with mankind, as he lieth with a woman, both of them have committed an abomination: they shall surely be put to death; their blood shall be upon them.

Lets face it, people are always going to find an excuse to do what they want to do. None can come up with a simple explanation to why such abominations are justified. They have to find excuses, and come up with lies in order to "protect themselves", while denying the truth of the matter. Now, I must say, as there is so much gays in this world, that will certainly be angry with me over my truth, even the truth that the Most High has given me through scripture, many will need to understand that you should not hate me for telling the truth, hate yourselves for not accepting the truth. The truth is the truth, and I am comfortable debating, knowing I am confident in all that I say. Ultimately this is no debate but a honest fact that is going to be one sided. This is not in hate, but in truth, and to wake up the lost sheep of Israel. Those who belong to the Most High, and need to find their way back to the Shepherd. For all those that say, "I was born gay, and this is the way that god made me", let me tell you this, the Most High is not a YAH (GOD) of confusion, and has no need to bring you into this world in such a way that will not gain you in any form of future life, and generations behind you, meaning children. If we were all born gay, as you claim, we would end life the moment we were all created, for your life will never carry on, and even life itself would not exist. For there is no ratio of straight, and gay being born. Some can't be born gay, while some straight. That's like saying evolution is now evolving, or should I say declining, due to the new species of faggots. Just won't happen, for there is no evolving, but declining, and it will never be a positive. We are all given the same, and the same is to deal with what you are, to create that which comes naturally. Male, and female, formed together on purpose to create life, and continuous life.

When one goes against nature, there is confusion, and hate, as well as, low self-esteem, and rebellion. All the signs that you are doing something wrong. Even further, sickness is formed through diseases, which is a major sign that you are jeopardizing your life, and the lives surrounding you, just based off of actions that are against nature. If you were to sleep with a man, being a man, you are not going to reproduce any form of baby. A seed and a seed, only make a filthy mess, while a seed and an egg, creates an embryo. Take a look at a plug that goes into the wall. Even electronics tell us through nature, how things work. When you plug your plug into the wall, you must use a male end to go into the female portion of the socket. Likewise when you put a headphone jack into a cell phone. It must be a male, and a female or else it just will not work.

So, with all said, and proven in facts, let me now explain why I believe homosexuality is a mental illness. The mind should be basic for all. As we have the common sense to understand the basics, which is 1-2-3, A, B, C, we must understand how we must pair man with women in order for life to continue, while hoping to remain healthy, and strong. We should know that all those who do not understand this "basic", must have something wrong with their brain. The mind is a powerful thing, and one who thinks something in right, in their own mind will believe just that, that it is right, however, that same mind can lie to itself without accepting the truth, within reality. If you are denying that male and female is necessary to reproduce, you are denying reality, and truth. And so, the truth is not in you, for you are not accepting the fact that you are living in reality. The truth, works, and backs up itself, while proving it can give examples. You must understand, by nature everything is formed, and operates correctly. There is no error in between. There is no fault in nature, but perfection, and guidance. Nature teaches us, so all we have to do is continue to follow nature, and we will be guided in the right direction. Again, to me, "nature" is the Most High, giving us understanding through example. If the example was not there, we would all be confused and living in a state of confusion that consist of not knowing which way to turn, nor how to operate the basics. Building would never be established properly, for we would just accept whatever its built. Homosexuality is a mental illness for it proves that one cannot have the basic understanding of nature, and without nature (The Most High), there is no way.

Those who are still trying to ignore and deny facts, they are living by choice, and not by nature. They are living selfish, and doing all for self-gain. They are also spreading disease, while not caring for Humankind. I believe such people are an abomination, confused, and ultimately have mental illness. The sad part about it is, the government is promoting such illness as normal, and polluting the masses, by allowing this mental illness to be as normal. If you know better, do better. If you have understanding, understand in full. If you seek knowledge, seek it out in full. If you refuse to accept the truth, continue to live your lie, while the lie will not benefit you at all, which proves you hate yourselves, and your life is as nothing but confusion. The lies can't build a proper foundation, and only destroys itself, due to lack of purity.

Homosexuality is a mental illness, and for those who disagree, are most likely apart of the gay agenda that this government has been promoting ever since they took aim at the manly men of this planet, including trying to destroy the Messiah, and introducing science to debunk the Most High. All of which is apart of the gay agenda.

CHAPTER
2

THE GAY AGENDA
(IT'S ALL TAINTED, THEY CORRUPT EVERYTHING)

This topic is something that I have been touching on for quite some time now, and as they expose themselves, it is quite clear that this agenda is in full effect. Though, they treat this illness as they treat the fake Jews, where you cannot even mention anything about them, or you will face the consequences. As you may have witnessed, certain celebrities were labelled as "anti-Semitic", and were forced to apologize, and even lose their job. This has been going on for quite some time, and the funny thing about it (sarcastically), is it typically remarks being made usually by an Israelite, (Black, African American, Negro) all of who are the real Jews upon this earth, being YAH (GOD) chosen people. On top of that, they lost their jobs due just giving an opinion on the fake Jews. This is the same establishment that they are creating for the gays. For those who speak badly upon homosexual, even being a simple opinion, they are forced to face a lot of backlash, and depending on the business that they do, position title, or ranking, they get punished as the "gay mafia", demands an apology.

I remember posting online a few videos touching on such topics of homosexuality, and was first warned for hate speech, and then kicked off and banned from the sites for future post. It's censored living. It seems like it is on every subject that is happening right now. Even if you were to speak on the virus that happened in 2019 called Coronavirus. They, the government doesn't want nobody to speak on such things, even though these things have affected everyone. Likewise with the wars going on. They are trying to hush everything. Wars are happening everywhere, and as these gays came out of the closet in a wide range of people, roughly in 2002, they have been polluting the world. Commercials, television shows, and reality television, you would find a least one gay person included. As the media is the power machine for the government, they use this platform to fulfill their agenda. Making the world forcefully, and gradually accept them into our every days lives. It has come to the point that the majority of the world has turned gay, and it is spreading like a virus. If you noticed as I have, many celebrities that are not gay, would say, "I have no hate for them, and am not against them", yet they claim to be believers in Christ. Some are just so afraid of speaking their mind, that they do not want to offend them. Some are bound by contract with Satan, to push and promote such evil, and will get punished for anything they say again the temporary powers that be. With proof of such things, there was a singer caught on camera with a transgender, and another singer/rapper said something joking in a disrespectful manner again him, and ended up having to wear a dress in public, while having perm. It shouldn't be hard for your to figure out who that rapper is. I look at other rappers out there that set trends for the youth, and corrupt the minds, hoping to benefit off of of doing such things financially. Take for example, when gangster rap was too violent for people to accept, and many people became scared. Other rappers would now take over, while promoting homosexuality, and they got that push, even while not claiming to be gay. As you have witnessed in roughly 2003-2005, there were rappers wearing pink, and toning down the gangster movement, and other rappers as well that claimed to be gangsters, doing manicures, and as they got their finger nails done, and permed hair, they were more-less putting on an act, while claiming to be pimps. Such things were homosexual activities, and they would rather now act than to be real, which is why you can still see those doing such things still in the music industry, and prospering. Those rappers would kiss other men on the lips, and say, "no-homo", as if that gave them a pass to do such gay things. That to me is weirdo stuff, and is considered gay regardless. There is no pass just because of words alone. That term "no-homo" went on for a couple years, while it was heard all around the streets. People doing gay things, while using that term to avoid being labelled as gay. Just goes to show you the power of the tongue, and how these rappers, and such can manipulate the masses to believe such things that can harm the existence of many.

Well, as a book author, but before being an author, a man in the truth, that is not afraid to tell it like it is, and expose the ways of the wicked, as well as have no fear is speaking my mind, and upholding my beliefs in perfect religion. If you do not agree, all you can do is either hate me, or come back with some form of opinion that I do not have to agree with at all. It's just so terrible to know that so many soft people out here, don't want their feelings hurt, and want you to believe in what they believe in, or they end up hating you, and make you an enemy. This is my opinion. It's the same thing that I can argue over, in gays not wanting to be straight. Yet, I let people live the lives that they choose, and take no offence. I'm not the one bending over, and taking it up my backside. I'm definitely not the one getting down on my knees, while facing another man. That's y'all. If anything the offence should be placed upon you by your own doings.

The thing that I do not like about this agenda, is that they are forcing us all to accept them. It's disrespectful, for they make sure to not allow those in their religion to express their religion without backlash, yet we should all just accept this form of illness into our lives, which also goes against our beliefs. They ban our religions in school, while they take away from the foundations that so many have been grown up on. Yet, they now introduce such evil into the schools, and in the workplace, as well as in public places. When last have you seen the KKK posting up in a bus freely? It would get a lot of negative attention. Likewise if I were to put up Scripture verses around the place, especially schools, they would take them down immediately. Likewise with the Black Panther Party, promoting more truth. Yet, they post gay flags all over the place. They support this movement so much, due to wanting world depopulation. They know that by being gay, less people will have children, and having less children, means less people in this earth, and more space for the rich to play golf, as well as it would be easier to manipulate and control the world itself, while having more rebellious people that accept sin, instead of those with morals and values.

I look at women empowerment. Another push by the government. Equality for women all around the world. Which is fine to an extent. My only thing is, if that is the push that they desire, treat all women as men. If you are in a warehouse, lift the heavy boxes likewise, and without help. If you are on a bus, stand up, if it is crowded, and give up your seat once in a while. Still, this is a one sided battle, for as a man, knowing women are not equal in strength, nor in the workplace, I would still be a gentleman and give up my seat when it's crowded and I see a female, or an elderly person, and of course a child. Women empowerment is a huge step in homosexual, for it is the breaking down of the manly man. Those who now have to accept females giving orders, and being in charge, within certain sectors that we work in. Many will not accept it. I remember being in a similar position. Working under a female within a company that decided to exercise such rights. As she was supervisor, she took it on herself to play the role of a butch, and a "butch" to me, as a dike female that wants to come off manly. She will try her best to be pushy, disrespectful, and want power, while taking advantage of the men. The thing about trying to be something, doesn't make you something, and with that said, you fake the reality of what it is. Nobody liked her, and it was an unpleasant place to work. I quit, knowing it wasn't for me, as I am an alpha male. As she would talk down to people, I couldn't allow that to happen to me, and we clashed a bit, until it was just unacceptable. Not to say that females in charge of things, must be a square, but by being respectful, and humble. I can live next door to anyone, and work with anyone, just as long as respect is present. Many do not want to keep, nor uphold such common courtesy practices.

Role reversal is something that is happening as well. Many men are now taking on roles of the women. Such things are also promoted by the government. Within the media, you can witness, how many television shows have the housewife, now being held by the man, who is supposed to be the husband. It starts with television, and movies. It is promoted within reality television, and as it is promoted, the woman becomes the head of the household, and are comfortable being the pants wearers, not just because of random things, but for the fact that women now bring in more money for the household, and who ever has most money, typically call the shots. Real men, know to keep the household in check, and do not care for money based relationships. Personally, I would never want to be second to a spouse (wife). That just will not happen. For there were times in the dating areas that certain females I was with, felt overpowered due to making more money. They would mention that they make more money, and how much things costs to operate. Creating a nasty image for themselves, which made me end things quickly. If you need to tell me how much bills cost, and how much you are paying for mortgage/rent, as well as how much money you are making, that is a turn off, especially if I have my own, and may just be visiting. Not due to jealousy in any form of way, but due to the fact that those females I dated were only stating such things to show off, and to feel like I must comply to their demands, or else. So, "or else", was me making the smarter choice in not dating them at all, and moving on.

Speaking on "dating", the game don't wait and has played a major role in not only taking away the manly man, but destroying the woman due to being egotistical. Women have become less and less attractive throughout the years, not due to looks, but due to having big heads, and being picky, having high standards, and expecting too much, as well as their inner parts are not desirable, meaning their mind, and heart, and in some cases, their privates parts being polluted. They have been promoted as a gift to man, and has been given too much attention by many men, some of which who were seeking wives, but for those who have been seeking a wife, especially online, they have gotten so much attention that they have too many options, and that is a toxic thing, for what person would want to just chose one, when you can sift through many. Many have become so gassed up. They have become undesirable for many men, as for the same reason that no real men, is going to wait on a bench to be selected, and no real man, is going to pursue a female, as if she is worth more than himself. If you are not looking to be equal, you are not going to be desirable by any real man. I know this for a fact, knowing I would never want to date a woman, while she has many numbers in her phone, while dating them too. There is a code of ethics, and morals, which I follow and keep. If I were to have many females, even one other in my phone, while dating one, it would be considered cheating, and so, we should all play the "game" fair. Yet, these females have so many numbers, and names of guys that are interested in them. The moment, you slip up or do not have what she is looking for, she will move on to the next one, and as I've personally experiences such things, she would come back, hoping to have her place in line, while not realizing, once you place a real man on the bench, we get up, and we leave. Hell no, Would I stick around, and wait for you to date other men, while hoping to be the apple of your eye. With all said and done, that turned me off, just to know that the land is polluted, and I would never want to waste my time on females that are not sincere, nor have morals/values for themselves. How can I respect that? It's not like they are virgins.

SCRIPTURE
Jeremiah 3:1
King James Version

1 They say, if a man put away his wife, and she go from him, and become another man's, shall he return unto her again? Shall not that land be greatly polluted? But thou hast played the harlot with many lovers; yet return again to me, saith the LORD.

These women most likely been with a handful, or even two handfuls of men, and defiled themselves, before dating you. To me, that is not attractive, and so, even I decided to remain single, until the Most High sends me who that prize female. As I just mentioned, "even I decided to remain single", this plays a role in the mind of manly men, that we do not want to be with someone who is defiled, and even too loose, to the point they are with many men, or unfaithful, so right there, is another form of why other men may turn away from women completely, and seek other men. I would never do such things, for if I can't get with a female, I would just remain single, but for other men, some may dab into places with other men, and that is the start of homosexuality. Not to be vain, but I find myself to be attracted/handsome, and would have trouble finding a wife, even date at certain times in my life, however, knowing my worth, I knew that I was still in a better position than those who are unattractive. Imagine how hard it must have been for them, knowing, I rate myself much higher? Just goes to wonder why those men, may have switched sides.

SCRIPTURE
Zephaniah 3:1
King James Version

1 Woe to her that is filthy and polluted, to the oppressing city!

As the government is promoting such homosexuality in schools, they are trying to corrupt the children. For what they teach, is what is crucial to the minds of the children. As you should know, before the age of twelve, the child is programmed with the teachings of whatever, whomever teaches that child, and it will stay with that child, until they grow older.

SCRIPTURE
Proverbs 22:6
King James Version

6 Train up a child in the way he should go: and when he is old, he will not depart from it.

As you can see within the Scripture verse above, "train up a child in the way that he shall go", and that says it all. If you give a child information of "acceptance", they will feel comfortable down the line, thinking that being homosexual is acceptable, and even worse, an option. As so you can understand my message that homosexuality is a mental illness, so they are programming the children to accept this illness within their lives, and when they grow older, they will think that it is normal. It's disturbing to witness such things today and age. It makes you wonder, why are they pushing such illnesses around more than any other things, that actually make sense? For example, "hate". Hate is real, and many people hate. Yet, they want to promote "love" while they do not promote YAH (GOD). When those who believe, understand that love is YAH (GOD). Without love, there is no YAH (GOD), and without the Most High, there is no love. So, instead of teaching true love, they are teaching "love is love", and that includes homosexuality. I would never have imaged to picture so much gays not just come out of the closet but sport their behaviour all around the world to this degree. I've witnessed many gay couples walking around, and even transgender, which is a topic I will touch on more within the chapters to come.

As I touched on the topic of "breaking down the manly man", I must say that this is happening, and even technology plays a major role in this gay agenda. For many men that used to use their hands, are now being replaced by robots. Manly men used to feel secure, while being crafty with their hands, but as automation came into play, there is no use for the worker with the hands, knowing the process is faster with machines. If you shake men's hands today, you can tell the difference from a few decades ago. From a firm handshake, to now, feeling like you are touching a dead corpse in your hands, is the feeling that I've felt while shaking hands with them that have weak frail hands. There is no might in them, and they are weaker than ever. They have not done anything physical, nor manly to earn such strong hands. Being a bodybuilder, I keep a good form, and when ever I shake someone's hands, I give a firm grip, not just to show respect, but to show who is the alpha male. Once I feel a man touch my hand, within a handshake, and it is weak, I feel disrespected, and it comes off gay, as I have to immediately release that persons hand, knowing I feel as if I am going to break it, and it's too soft for my liking. They should have never stuck their hand out in the fist place.

Everything feels tainted, and corrupt, since the government has played a major role in this "homosexual gay agenda". Everything good, they have been polluting. I look at the rainbow itself, and see how beautiful it is, while now, I can't look at it the same, knowing they, the "powers that be", has made the rainbow their logo, which is fruity (gay). There is nothing wrong with the rainbow, but they used it as a way to display their homosexuality, even destroying some colours that the Most High has created, just to benefit themselves.

S C R I P T U R E
Revelation 10:1
King James Version

1 And I saw another mighty angel come down from heaven, clothes with a cloud: and a rainbow was upon his head, an his face was as it were the sun, and his feet as pillars of fire:

Homosexuality is now everywhere, and in everything. As you can witness my book cover, it is a picture that I came across with an eagle on the end of the flag, with the flag itself being lit on fire, as it burns. Now, as the eagle represents America, in where I believe homosexuality started from, being Babylon, which is the route to all evil. This is where they get away with a lot of sin, while calling it "law", all of which is an abomination, for they would never get away with this in foreign countries. The people within the communities would rally together, go straight to where that homosexual lives, and put him/her out of the house and stone them to death. This government within the United States/Canada pushes such agendas, and first sets the trend for many other nations to fallow. You take a look musical artist, and those that come out of the closet, being most from North America, they become praised, and glorified for just being gay, and proud. Some selling out for the fame, while not even being gay, but promoting it as "normal", just to make some money off of it.

I again think about the workplace, and how men tend to do manly things, and as I mentioned with butch females, there are men that do not mind working in weaker areas, while sitting around with the females gossiping, and spreading rumours about others. They join assembly lines, and do work that is designed more for females. This government of "equality", was more designed for homosexuals, rather than equality for Blacks, who were here since the beginning. For those who are seeking work, needed quality in the workforce, when it came to pay, and opportunity itself. It had nothing to do with doing weaker roles, but advanced roles, that all were qualified to do. Yet, the government would rather support weaker men, complaining about the real manly men work, and take away from building strong men.

Overall the agenda to accept homosexuality is one of the main goals for the government, and they have succeeded. Many people now have problem with gays surrounding them, nor getting a gay best friend for certain females that felt by "following trend" would make themselves cool, and acceptable to talk to another guy, while hanging out with gay men, to feel like they can get a pass while talking to a straight man. I remember meeting a female, who would use that same excuse to get away, and talk to another man. Just because the guy is claiming to be gay, I don't accept that into my life, nor would I allow my spouse to mingle with any other man, so that ended as soon as it started.

This agenda has not only forced people to accept them, but to also have no choice but to respect their ways. Now, personally, I don't care if you want to be gay, however, I know it is not right, and I would never accept them into my life, nor feel like I can give them a pass, while going against my morals, and values that were established, to know right from wrong. Again, I have no gay friends, male, nor female.

I have no gays living among me. I have no gays that I work with, even if I did, I would not acquaint myself with them. For I remember one job with one homosexual supervisor, and I had to quit, due to just hearing that voice, which is put on and so sissy. It's toxic. There is not female that I've dated that I've allowed to have a gay friend, for that is disrespectful to me, and my morals. Imaging marrying that female, to have her invite her homosexual friend, and having that person be her "best friend", wearing a dress, instead of pants. That would never sit well with me. If you can avoid such things, do just that.

The government knows exactly what they are doing, and as it is not in schools, it is being taught everywhere and promoted in the media everywhere, and most importantly, in the music industry, which has the most influence possible, it is being played in the ears of the innocent children. We must stop this agenda, by not accepting it into our lives. We must stop this agenda, by monitoring what our children listen to. We must even take our children out of the public school that promote such garbage. Without doing so, we accept it. We allow our children to sit next to, and become friends with such people that are not normal, but in fact, dealing with mental illness.

CHAPTER
3

RAISED SOFT
(SOME MEN DO NOT WANT TO BE MEN)

Have you ever witnessed a homosexual male talk as a women? Have you ever witnessed one try to walk as a woman, and do womanly gestures with their body/hands/stance? I have, and I will tell you that it is disgusting to look at, and even hear. I despise such men for their weak ways, and cowardly lifestyles. Most men that turn gay, or should I say, choose to become gay, have gave up trying to be men. They do not want to be manly men. Some want to be women so badly, they do not mind being weaker, and taking on the roles of women, hoping to offer a man such things as a woman can. They are in fear of other alpha males out there, such as myself, and hate to be in competition with us real men. Some are raised by their mother, who is not strong, and may just play a major role in that child's life, teaching them such things that men should never be apart of. When you think about effeminate men, they are typically doing things that women tend to do, and have been trained in a way to feel like that lifestyle is acceptable. As mentioned before within the scripture verse, "raise a child in the way he shall go". For those men that are comfortable in such ways, are not going to care for what manly men think, knowing they were raised to be effeminate. The ways that they have, is womanly attributes, like gossiping, backbiting, whispering, being nosy, spreading rumours and lies, and even sabotage, and arguing instead of fighting with the fist. They use their tongue to do much damage. Instigating much problems between others. Being apart of every gossiping situation. Those who find pleasure in watching television shows with much dramas, and gossiping shows that no man should ever feel comfortable watching, even while sitting next to a female friend. They partake in feminine things, like manicures, facials, and caring a little bit too much about their own appearance. Spending a bit too long in the mirror. Putting on women's clothing, and this may not be in full, but in partial, like having a purse, or wearing tight tights, or short shorts. To me, those who wear ear, nose, and tongue piercings, have already gone too far. Men should never want to do such things, nor depend on such things to make them more attractive. I believe the women is the one that should be flattering, and charmed up.

Let me touch back on parenting. As many mothers that are obviously women, would do womanly things, they would have a boy child, and allow him to join in on those activities. This is a dangerous thing. Cooking, is acceptable. Cleaning is also acceptable. When it comes to sewing, and sitting around talking about other people, they need to refrain from such things. Allowing your child to sit around and gossip with you, and be too nosy, while being a busy-body in other people's business, is toxic. It's even worse when the boy's father is involved as well, and even comfortable with such things. For I've come across many weak men that are not the head of the household, but the following, and comfortable being the skirt wearer. Allowing their wives to take control, and give the orders. All while standing behind her with their hands in their pocket, or should I say, tail in between their legs, while their wives tend to handle any form of altercations, and situations. Such cowards. I recall a few times this happened, where the men would stand behind the female, while allowing the female spouse to mouth off, and take on the male, who is either attacking, or under attack, verbally, and physically. They would not say a thing, but stand behind their spouse, smiling, while she is blabbing off her mouth. Even one time, where a guy on a train was so pissed off over a situation that this guys spouse created, and she was aiming hard at this guy, while he kept trying to communicate with the man. Instead of him saying something, he stood there, and ended up getting beat up, knowing the real man, didn't want to take it out on the female. That guy that got beat up deserved it, knowing he should have manned up, and handled the situation, instead of remaining quiet. If you are a smaller dude, you do not have to fight, but at least speak, and that guy was not mute.

There are many men out there that should never have had children, especially boys children. Being a father is a important task, and one should be able to raise their child strong, while taking this role seriously. Without being strong yourself, not just physical, but mentally, and emotionally, without being emotion, you can certain damage your child's life. How can any father be comfortable with a gay/homosexual son? How can you allow that into your household?

How can you defend your son when you do not know how to be a man? I will tell you, if it is your wife that control the scene, you may as well squat to piss, and wear the apron in the kitchen, while doing the dishes. As mentioned in the chapter before this, women empowerment played a major role, and that role is having more power than the man. As much influence it can have on her husband, it can also be likewise unto any boy children. Having more money, made the women call the shots, and make weaker men, feel intimidated. Picture having a son, and your wife runs the household, what is your son going to expect to seek out in a mate? Of course, a stronger woman, that can pamper him.

One story that I never can stop speaking about, nor forgetting is a story of a childhood friend, who was causing strife with another kid, and that kid's father was there to witness, while telling his son, "fight him", while not engaging himself. As he sat back and watched his son fight my childhood friend, he was confident in his child. As his son, lifted up my childhood friend, and slammed him on the floor, on occasion. This kid, had the teaching from his parent, to man up, and handle it, which is positive. Nothing taken away from my childhood friend, for even in a loss, he took a win, for fighting, and not running his mouth, without backing it up, again even in a loss, he came out a real one. To that kids father, I tip my hat to him, and I can assure you, not knowing twenty too thirty years later, that kid, has grown into a man, however, which way he turned out. I can assure you, being gay most likely would not be an option, compared to other kids that had sissies for parents.

To those who were not raise weak while choosing to be gay, they are worse then the children that were raised to be gay, for they just do not want to be men. If there is sports teams in school that individuals would rather not get hurt, and become a cheerleader on the sidelines. There are parents out there that may have done all that they can do for their child, and that child, just wanted to be weaker by being homosexual. That homosexual child, will grow up, behaving in ways that will only expose themselves as filthy, and weak. It's one thing to actually have an excuse, while having parents that raised you soft, but for those who actually had no excuse, and wanted to live as homosexual, is an abomination.

There are men out there that are married with children, and they just do not want to be men. They would rather be victims, and not want to "man up" in any situation. Instead, they feel comfortable most while having someone else support them, and fight their battles. How can you even call yourself a man? I've seen men do just that, I couldn't have looked at them any worse than sissies. What a disaster. I wrote a book called "What Happened to the Manly man?", and for those who want to touch more on this subject, by all means pick up a copy, for you will find some interested facts within it.

Now and days, if you have a war with men, they will deny having any problems with you, just to avoid any static (conflict). They would rather deny it, and sit home doing witchcraft/sorcery on you, while living in fear. They would doing telepathy, just to get a message across you. Believe it or not, this is true. Not in my lifetime would I ever expect such cowardly men out here doing such things. I mean, sitting behind an evil device, while running their mouth, and hiding away. That is beyond low. Once you see how technology is being used to weaken the men, as well as strengthen them in a weak way, by getting away with things that they no longer have to face. Just take a second to think about that. Think about a guy that you had issues with, actually talking to you telepathically? What is the first thing that you would think about when it comes to that guy? For me, he would be labelled as a punk, a sissy, a faggot, and major coward, just to name a few. Back in the days it was better to just get beat up, and still have that respect, rather than to do such weak things unto another man. I would even respect a group of men fighting one person, even though that is weak, I still respect it, because that individual that got beat up, can certainly find them one by one, and handle his business. But, to hear a guys voice talking to you telepathically, that is a no, no. Even worse, to try and talk tough, how pathetic, and unbelievable. Never in my years upon this earth, would I ever want to take that route. Never have I had someone I feared that much, to be so weak, to even contemplate such weak ways. Such a shame, yet this is happening around the world.

I look at how weak men are being handled in this world today. They are so fragile emotionally that it is sickening. I'm sick and tired of hearing emotion men bitch, and complain. I'm so annoyed at grown men, whining more than women. It's not a good look when they are comfortable speaking too long, and wanting much attention, while even gossiping about others. I've also witnessed many men gossiping on a daily basis, putting matters that didn't even concern them, as their top priority for the day, and weeks, and years. Something is truly wrong with them, and it's all due to programming.

I was at work the other day and was happy to say unto the coworkers that I was with, how fascinating it is to have ultimate fighting going on, and rough sports. I like such things for boys, knowing that in the last decade, men have adapted more to technology, sitting in one spot, doing nothing with themselves. As you can look on the book cover, from the book, "What happened to the Manly Man?", you can see the work out equipment. As a bodybuilder, I get a lot of looks as if I am an endangered species. Something that many people rarely see anymore due to the lack of care for self. Not many care to work out, and to get in shape, as well as build their muscles. The cell phone, is toxic unto many people, and a distraction majorly. As I'm single and have no children, I find it saddened that I could not give the best to any seed of my own. For I would be more than happy to raise up a child in a positive way, while being the example as a grown adult male, who is traditional, and real. I can never allow a son to be raised weak, but strong, and while investing time into a child, I would do my best to make sure he would be better than me, stronger than me, and raised right, so that being homosexual is never an option. As some parents do not allow their children to fight, and the discipline factor is no longer there, it takes away from raising them right, and structured on a foundation that is built to last.

S C R I P T U R E
Proverbs 19:18
King James Version

18 Chasten thy son while there is hope, and let not thy soul spare for his crying.

Sometimes it takes a belt to raise a child right. Sometimes it take firm speaking. Anything less, would only allow that child to be raised soft, and that is not a good thing. Many parents talk nicely to their child and say that they do not believe in spanking/harsh discipline, but that is a reason for them to remain soft. If you are having trouble raising a child in the right way, due to yourself even being too soft, and you want to change that, start off in the gym. Light weights. You can even go for walks, and allow your child to be one with nature. For nature helps us through many trials, once you respect nature. Remember, nature will teach you, and as I reference nature to the Most High. As I believe that if you can raise your child right, and do the right things, being manly, as construction, building things, using their hands on power tools, and being physically, in training to fight, or be in competitions with rewards for strength.

Speaking of being raised soft, I think about adoption, and argue the fact that homosexuals should never be allowed to adopt. It is confusion to any child out there to have two of the same sex, as parents, especially while adopting from a young age. As I feel that homosexuals are not mentally capable of having their own mind right, how is it possible for them to raise a child up? I've heard stories of children that grown up to be adults, speak on their adopted parents, and say, "they took me in while my real parents gave up on me, and my adopted parents cared for me, so I don't care if they are gay". There is something with that saying that I've heard a few times, knowing "being nice", and comparing it to morals and values, are two different things. Anyone can be nice. Anyone can be good towards another, however, mistaking "good" with sin, is damaging. Having an adopted child adapt to a lifestyle that is an illness, is foul. For those adopted children will all most likely say the same things. They will continue to say how great their parents are, however, not seeing the wrong within the picture frame. If you are raising anyone to be something, they will be just that. If you allow a child to see and witness certain walks of man, that child will eventually walk the same, for that is the way of teaching, especially when it comes to parents, and mentors. If all parents today were to raise their child to think it is okay to smoke weed, they will eventually pass the blunt unto their child, and he/she will not reject it. For that is something that that child has been witnessing for the longest time. I've even seen this happen as a Chinese child was drinking liquor. That kid must have been five years old, and behaving normal. That boy's parents must be comfortable with it as well, knowing they have pictures of this boy online doing such that without any form of restraint.

As I continue to say, homosexuality is a disease, I completely disagree with those being gay/lesbian, ext raising children. No child should grow into a lifestyle that is corrupt, and feeling as if it is the normal ways of reality. They will certainly accept it, for they think that it is love, but it is not. It is two men, or two women that just do not want to accept living righteous. They do not want to take on the reality of the fact that they can never have children together as homosexuals, and will have no choice but to rely on adoption, or the tools from another to create the job. I look as lesbians that are homosexual. Even some known dikes that fight in ultimate fighting, that sport around "their" child that they created together through science. They had to rely on a strangers sperm in order for them to make one of themselves pregnant. That child doesn't belong to the homosexual "lover", but unto the stranger of the donor. Likewise when men think that it is acceptable to adopt, and sport "their" child, as well as use their sperm to pay off a female to have the child for them. They need to rely on adoption, or that donor as well, to continue their lie. They need to find ways to feel "normal", while not caring for nature's natural order, way, and teachings. Tell me an adopted child that was raised by homosexuals to grow older, and tell the truth about homosexuals? Tell me one that is not okay with their ways, and does not love them. "That's my dad, and my other dad", is that what they would say to their peers, without being looked upon as weirdos, while feeling embarrassed? Not in this day and age. It's sadly normal.

No matter how much people accept homosexuality, they can't deny facts, and the truth. So walk with your shame, while the truth, even within nature of the world tells of reality. Without shame, there is no class, and without class, there is no level of self-respect.

CHAPTER
4

GAY AND PROUD, BUT NO SHAME

I like to look at the definitions of words, and as I came across the term "gay", they describe it as being "happy", and then I looked up the word proud, and found out that it meant to feel too favoured, and honourable. If you put those two words together, you get that "gay and proud" means, "happy to be honoured, and favoured. Now, if you double back, and look at what I wrote before about certain music artist that come out of the closet and claim to be homosexuals, tend to have higher careers than other artist that are not gay. They are being honoured, and favoured by Satan, being the media, and the dark-side. Those artist are happy to collect the fame and fortune that comes along with it. They are doing the work of the devil, and should never feel to happy. You tell me, how can one walk the streets knowing he took it up his backside? That to me is a damn shame, and volunteering/consensual rape.

I relate such things to jail/prison, where men that have had gotten raped. They didn't have no form of happiness while getting raped, and proud is something that they were not. In fact, they were ashamed, and felt the shame upon them, knowing that they were robbed of manhood, and kept it on a "hush", hoping no one else would find out about it. Did they make it known to all that they endured such infliction? Of course not. Did they come out of the closet, no! Instead I bet you that those that it happened to would rather find a closet and remain in there if they could. Watching a few documentaries, I've heard stories of those that is has happened to, kill the person responsible. Not to go too deep into it, but when little boys are raped as children, their entire lives are messed up, and they tend to lash out more, due to being tainted. Again, this sick world has a lot of pedophiles, and are right in our faces, especially while watching television, for most actors, and those on television, owners of sports teams, and so on, are the same type of people that do such crimes as rape, and sadly get away with it, due to status. It's terrible, it's disturbing, and it is filthy. As they are only thinking about themselves, they do not care for that individual that has to live with such circumstances.

My point to bringing up rape within jail/prison,

and speaking such things, is to say this, those who have this mental illness called "homosexuality", should not be going around feeling comfortable, while being proud, and happy. You should feel just as those men who had their manhood taken away from them. Instead, I hear men out there, being very ignorant, and mouthy, while claiming to be gay. Most men that are gay, I've noticed had a "look at me" tendencies, and attitude. They speak louder, and perform as a woman, while trying to grab attention. They do not care that they are damaging Humankind, and carrying such diseases that can and has already killed many men, and women, gay, and straight.

The worst kind of gays out there, are those who claim to go both ways, while calling themselves "bi-sexual". There is no such thing. That's like calling yourself a transgender, yet was born with a penis. That would make you a man. You are a total fag, if you are sleeping with other men. While sleeping with women, you are only showing that you are trying to fit in with many people. When in truth, you are causing disease that are out there, that can harm straight individuals, men, and women.

For example, a man sleeps with a man, and gets a sickness upon him. Then one of those men, sleep with a woman, and transmit that disease onto her, while she then sleeps with another straight man, and that is how this shit spreads. Doesn't that sound like something that should be contained? To me it does, for if someone can die from it, it is a slow kill, and should be counted as murder. Where is the proud in that? Where is the happiness? Especially to the man that is straight, and had to get infected by a disease that you started, even while being straight himself?

I look at the gay parades, and as they claim to be "happy", have you ever witnessed such disgust? These people walk nearly nude out there on the streets, and show off themselves, while sporting the "rainbow" colours, and even adult toys strapped unto them. They prance around while cross-dressing, wearing wigs, and fashion that represents bondage. It's a sick way of living, and they all look scary, as clowns. I look at them, and even get upset, when they do dress like women, while corrupting straight men. We've all watched episodes of Jerry Springer, and witnessed so many men dressing as females cross-dressing, and lying to straight men about being women. The reaction of most men, is to attack the deceiver. Again, being another reason why most men, decide to not date anymore

Now and days, you can't even tell, due to make-up, or as I like to say, "fake-up", which is designed to trick and deceive. Such a shame. The natural beauty is something that is rarely seen anymore in women, and most women tend to use fake-up, which is overdoing it, and they come off as cross-dressing women likewise.

SCRIPTURE
Deuteronomy 22:5
King James Version

5 The woman shall not wear that which pertaineth unto a man, neither shall a man put on a woman's garment: for all that do so are abomination unto the LORD thy God.

My point to this is that, why do they show themselves in such a disgustinging manner? Why can't they just be who they are? Why must they cross-dress, and deceive? Again, touching back on the subject of men dressing like women, while lying to men about being women, when they are born men. It's selfish and disturbing. Any man doing such things, should be stoned to death. Reason why I say that this is a mental illness. How can you change your sex? It's impossible. Even if you cut off your penis, you will never be labelled as a women. Nor if you are a female that decides to wear any form of attire to make yourself appear as a man, you are still not a man. If you can't have respect for life, you can't even show that you even have respect for self. It's all confusion, and its lays within the mind of those who think that it is normal. Ask yourself, if you have to dress like a man, when you are a woman, likewise, if you have to dress like a woman, when you are a man, how can you be sane?

In my time, I've seen so many men try to dress like women, and they only come off crazy. I remember being on public transit one time, while with an ex-girlfriend of mine, who was my girlfriend at that time. There was a big Black guy, as big as me in a dress. This dude kept trying to get closer to me, while I was standing in the busy bus. As my girlfriend at the time noticed my reaction, she quickly stood in front of me, as I wanted to punch that guy out. The worst case scenario is that that guy beats me up, if I were to fight him, ha ha, but jokes aside, I would never lose, and make sure of it. As it seems gays have no limit to size of stature today, there are some big guys nowadays, that are homosexuals, and it's a shame to witness. Anyways, that guy on the bus, was lucky my ex stepped in, for I was seconds away from starting a fight with him, and the messed up thing about it is, I do not want to touch gay men, for I automatically picture them with disease, that may just spread unto others. If they scratch you, and or wrestle you, it can be a dangerous thing. It's like being attacked by an animal with rabies.

Have you witnessed how clean some of these homosexuals are in their living? They have "neat freak" ways about them, but little do they know they are the most filthy people upon the planet, even worse than hoarders. Most equivalent to swine, knowing a pig plays in his own shit. For those homosexuals choose to take it up their backside, and defile themselves. How clean is that? There is no shame. There is no cleanliness. Their is no safety. Be clean where it matters, and that is the brain. The mind is a powerful thing, and those who are gay, need to repent, while using their mind to find understanding.

To those men out there trying to force their homosexuality on others, have some shame. If you are going to be homosexual, do not force yourself on straight men, and women. Be gay, but find gay partner. Do not try to corrupt the straight, as you would not like for Christians to preach unto you about gay-awareness, as we as the straight do not want to be tempted by fags that can't stick to themselves. Do unto others as you would like others do unto you.

CHAPTER
5

LOVE IS LOVE?
NO!
GOD IS LOVE

SCRIPTURE
1 John 4:8
King James Version

8 He that loveth not knoweth not God; for God is love.

I'm sick and tired of hearing people say, "love is love", while supporting this gay agenda, and homosexuality. Love is not love. That is just another saying that makes people feel comfortable. Those who accept such gays, are not real people. They are not thinking straight, and are apart of the problem. There is no love in homosexuality. There is self-hate in homosexuality. There is disobedience in homosexuality. There is no morals, nor values in homosexuality. I repeat, there is no love in homosexuality. This is a sick and twisted lifestyle, for rebellious, and outlaw individuals. They are rejected by real people with morals and values. I respect the ways of those foreign countries that stone these heathen to death. They seek them out, and stone them, until they die. For that is what they deserve, for disrespecting life itself, and cutting off the way of the heathen, that can certainly spread unto others, especially the youth, to think that it is acceptable. They are going against nature, and going against the Most High. For the Most High intended good for the people. The world today is filled with sin, and those who are rebellious, are those who find pleasure in sin, while going against morals, and values. This is something that many people have accepted, and allowed to make sin, comfortable.

It's sickening to witness such abomination in the church, while gay pastors are out here preaching, and dividing the flock, while lying to the congregation. They are only doing what they want to do, in order for themselves to feel accepted. They care-less about the world, nor the people. For if they did, they would not join the church. I can't imagine what is said during Sunday service, for those who still follow the wrong day. If they are living sin, and doing one of the most evil things known to man, what are they talking about in the church, as pastors? They have nothing to say about repentance, when they are out there doing the worst and need to find repentance as well. For this same reason, many church goers are accepting lies, while not reading the Holy Scripture within the Bible, for themselves.

SCRIPTURE
Jeremiah 23:1
King James Version

1 Woe be unto the pastors that destroy and scatter the sheep of my pasture! saith the LORD.

Now, let me tell you something. Love as we know it is the Most High. We know this who believe. To those who do not believe, know not YAH (GOD), nor do they have any structure with a good foundation. These are people that rebel, and find pleasure in sin. As they live a life filled with confusion, they do not love themselves even. For if they did, they would have YAH (GOD) with them. They know not the Most High. So, when I hear about gay pastors in the church, they do not even know the Most High. Instead, they are mocking, and will not get any reward thereof.

These heathen homosexuals are nothing but confused. They hate themselves more than they hate anyone else. Most just rebel due to hating their parents. If you look at movies, they are portrayed as rebellious towards parents, and it's true. For that is how it starts.

They become ignorant, and have self-hate, while they are lost souls, hoping to find their way. These types of people, typically end up gothic. They indulge in the dark side, wear dark clothing, piece their body, and rebel. They even call themselves rebels, as they wear chains on themselves, and just come of as weirdos. Clearly a mental illness. No one is forcing them to be like this. They are lost, rejected, and can't fit in, because they are lost to themselves. If you love yourself, you take care of yourself. Not tattoo skulls on your body, and mark your skin, while living for the moment. That moment is in anger, and in rebellion, due to them not finding their way. These heathen, are upset at the world, and also typically end up doing a lot of drugs.

We must understand that there are people "living", while hating themselves, and wanting to commit suicide. They want to die, but are scared to. To me, these people are no good, because, they are trouble-makers. Most of them want others to feel sorry for them, or want others to accept them, when they don't even understand that they can't be accepted, when they are not showing their true selves.

They are showing a lie, and if someone were to accept them, they would only be ignorant, and accepting a lie into their lives.

The Most High wants what is best of HIS children, and would certainly want other nations to live in peace, and respect HIS world, for HE is the One who created it. All of us are guest here, and most are making a mockery out of this gift. It should be blessing to have life for all. For all have opportunity to do what ever they want to do, yet so many waste time, and even harm the lives of others, due to self-hate, and low-self-esteem.

It has gotten so bad for some men out here that took the route of homosexuality, that they are now desiring to be called "transgender". Even the sick way of parents that label their kid as "confused". How could that be? What went wrong with the minds of the people to allow this shit to happen? As I said already, "If you are born with a penis, you are a man, and if you are born with a vagina, you are a woman". There should never be an option after birth. Yes, there are some guys that develop breast, but that is due to fat, and being overweight.

Yes, there are some very unattractive females out there that are hard to look at, and even call "women", but they are. For those that look like a female, being men, cut your hair, do what is necessary to be a man. Lift weights. Likewise for the females who look like men. Just because you look like a dude, you don't have to dress like one, nor shave your head to appear as them.

SCRIPTURE
1 Corinthians 11:15
King James Version

15 But if a woman have long hair, it is a glory to her: for her hair is given her for a covering.

I remember one time while I was doing my laundry in a building that I lived in. There was a "confusion", that appeared as a man, even though that person was a female. Yet, respect is respect, and she was talking to me about the building. To me, she looked like a "Tom boy", and it was clear. Even another guy that came in said unto her, "she looks like boy", as she was interested in me, and he said that to basically allow her to know that she is not attractive. For me, all I was doing is my laundry, for I was not trying to get with her, and this is why "being nice" at times, can come off as "flirting", or "likeable", when in reality, by nature I'm just a good person, and it has nothing to do with flirting, nor being nice. Again, respect is respect. Nonetheless, her face could show that she was offended, yet said nothing. If you are a female that wants to be a man, take on the role of being a man, defend yourself, for I sure wasn't going to, because I agreed with him, but just never said it to her face, knowing I didn't need to rude, nor would it benefit me. I could truly care-less about her choices.

I never met an alien before. Yet, if they were friendly creatures that spoke English, it would still be an awkward conversation, knowing it's something that is not normal. Likewise, I feel the same towards homosexuals, for in my head, I automatically think of a guys taking it up their anus, or putting things in their mouth that should never go in the mouth of another man. I can't imagine a guy sleeping, cuddling up with another guy in bed together. Ewe. Most dudes is hairy all over, and to be holding one another, is disgusting, and mental illness. I do not even like touching a man, nor looking a man in his eyes for too long. When ever I take public transit, and see a seat available next to another man, I would rather stand, for no man should be that close unto another. Especially if your legs are touching another guys. Likewise, when a guy gets up out of the seat. I'm not so fast to take that seat, due to the heat that is on that seat from his body.

I'm going to keep this simple by saying it again, you do not know love, unless you know the Most High. If you are denying the facts about being rebellious, hateful towards women, maybe your mother and you had a disagreement, maybe even your father, I can assure you that you are not sane in the mind. Most men that turn gay have hate for their mother, and their father neglects them. There is no love there at all.

Love is not love when you put yourself in the line of danger. Love is not love, when you can get sick and die from being what you are. Love is not love, when you go against nature, and hate yourself in the process. Love is not love, when you can spread a disease unto another individual. Love is not love, when you cannot create something positive. Being HIV/AIDs positive, is not a positive thing.

CHAPTER
6

DISEASE CARRIERS
(AIDs HIV, AND MONKEY POX)

Another fact that is here, is that you cannot lay with another man, while being a man without risking your health when it comes to the bedroom. When a man and a man lay together, they have a high risk of catching some form of disease. While, the most that can happen between a man and woman, is that the women can get pregnant, which is much more beneficial in all angles, compared to catching a virus/disease that can ultimately kill you in the end. A child, is considered a blessing, if brought into this world, the right way. That child can be born and amount to something, if you didn't indulge in drugs, nor heavy alcohol, that can affect that child, that child will be alright.

I look at all the types of disease out there that are sexually transmitted. I would put pictures up in this book, but I truly can't stand to look at such things, knowing how disgusting it looks. Yet, I think it is best for those who are gay that may have no came across such illness before to witness. Take a look at these pictures. I just hope that you are not eating while reading this book, for you will certainly spit out all that you ingested. Here are light photos of those with HIV, AIDs, And STDs - Sexually Transmitted Diseases. For privacy, I have not included the full face image of those with such cases.

HIV

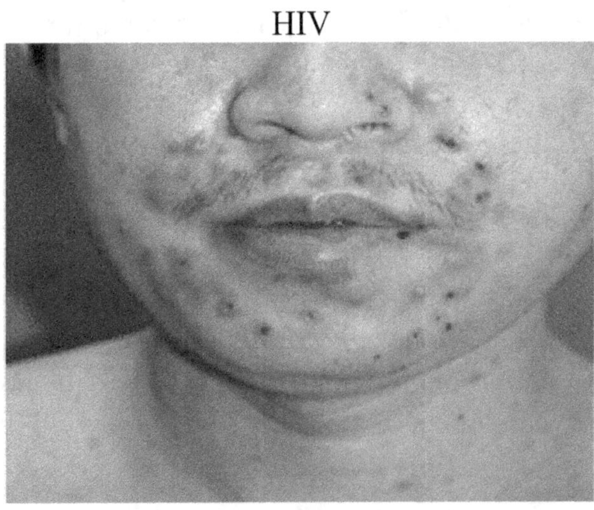

STD

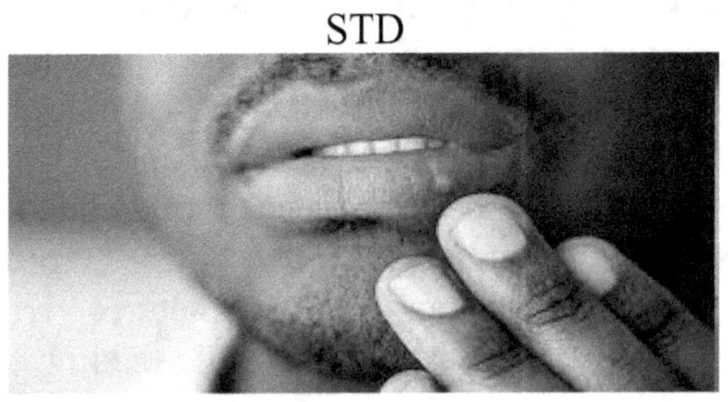

STD

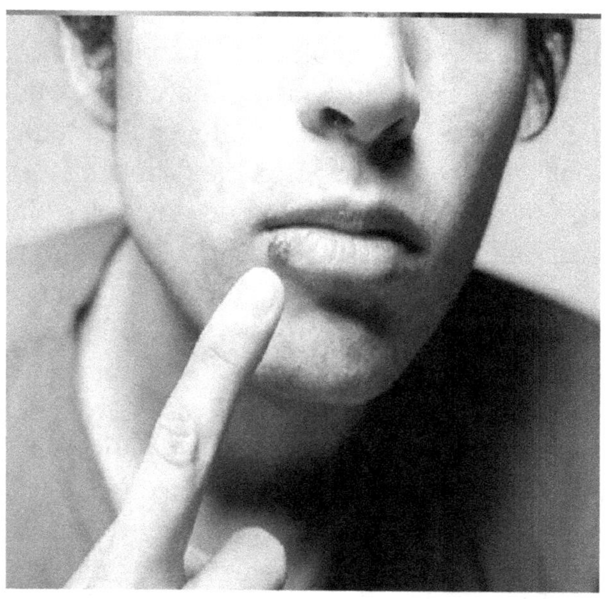

Now, these images were very light, compared to the search that I had to endure, while finding these. Yuk! I encourage you to not kiss anyone on the lips who have such faces. I've seen much worse online, however, this is a clear sign that someone is cheating, and spreading diseases to you. Even within a straight relationship. I suggest moving as I tend to move, and while dating females, I would not kiss until I knew she was clean. I would not even want to go further than that, as safety comes first. You never know. Some may say that they have a pimple, but pimples on your lip is not normal. Just saying that alone, would you not take such things into consideration? Don't you have any form of shame that you want to upkeep? For if you do not, you do not love yourself, nor your life, for a part of loving your life, is making sure you refrain from all sickness known to man, especially those that we have control over. That one moment can change your life, and the lives surrounding you. Now, just because the government is promoting such evil, that doesn't mean it is okay. We tend to follow things that are acceptable by man, but what about the Most High's laws, statues, and commandments?

Again, to those that think that they were born gay, and can't repent nor feel like they can't turn straight again, that is not true, and you are just living a lie with an excuse to continue to be filthy. For there is no temptation that can overpower you.

SCRIPTURE
1 Corinthians 10:13
King James Version

13 There hath no temptation taken you but such as is common to man: but God is faithful, who will not suffer you to be tempted above that ye are able; but will with the temptation also make a way to escape, that ye may be able to bear it.

Time is at hand, and as life goes on, so does the germs and new diseases that are formed. As 2022 is here, and going on to 2023, we have now been introduced to a new virus called, "Monkey Pox".

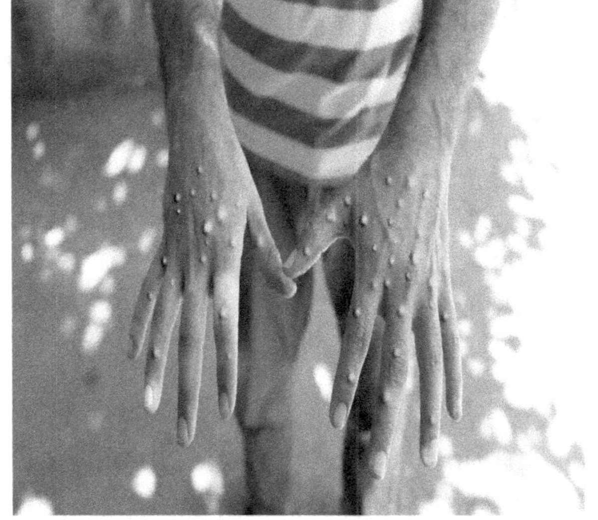

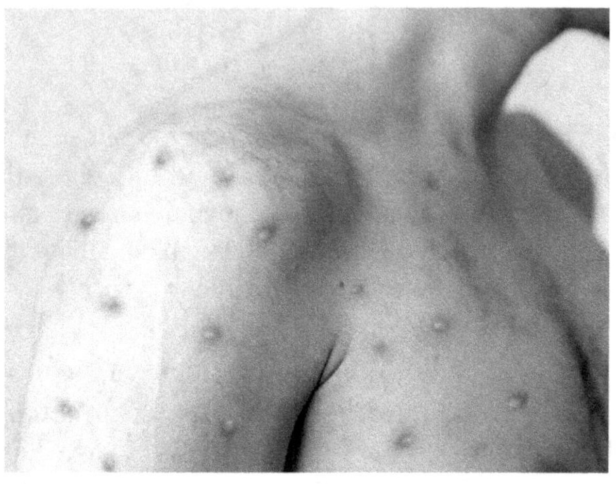

A virus that spreads from person to person, however, it was formed by the wickedness of man, while defiling themselves with one another. This is a warning sign from above. For mostly homosexuals are obtaining this disease, and it is nothing pretty. If you wanted to come out of the closet, or may just be still in there, now, it will certainly give you the red carpet treatment, as you can't hide such a illness.

As you can also witness through these photos, men, that appear guy by their attire, wearing short shorts, and tight clothing, while waiting to get the vaccine. All due to the filthy ways of men.

Still got pride?

CHAPTER
7

THE WORST KIND OF HOMOSEXUALS, ARE THE LONELIEST, BITTER HOMOSEXUALS

When you think about the "go along, get along gang", you think about followers of man. You think about being accepted, and being able to fit in with everyone. That is how it goes for the homosexual mental illness community. There are those who actually still can't fit in, and those who are exposing their mental illness of homosexuality, are single homosexuals that just can't find a gay lover. They can't find friends, they have no form of acquaintances, and become bitter. As they witness the harsh reality of their choices, they are now even more angry that no one wants them in their life, including their parents, and no other homosexual, as they would desire. I think about straight men who cannot find dates, and those are typically the most bitter and lonely people, as though I thought, until this wave of homosexuals appeared, and then they took the place of the worst, for they are angry when they cannot find "love". They are rebellious to parents, and hate their existence, while behaving as if they should be given some kind of award, and special treatment.

They are the loud, angry homosexuals that

tend to look attention, and hope for all people to "LOOK AT ME, LOOK AT ME", type emotions, while causing much trouble. They rebel more often than the others that are gay. Touching back on straight people that end up alone, and bitter, while comparing it to those lonely homosexuals. The straight lonely man goes through life while having no hope whatsoever, while witnessing life pass them by as years go by, right before their face. They see age play a factor, and their un-attractiveness becomes worse as they get older. No one wants them, and no one wants to even communicate with them, while they crave someone in their life. Instead, most tend to turn angry, and bitter towards the world, and people in general. Some turn to rape. Likewise for the homosexual that has devoted his life to this mental illness of claiming they like men over women, while no men want them. Yet, the majority of this population is homosexual, and they still find it hard to find "love". So, imagine someone rebellious compared to that straight individual that just wants love, and can't find it, but turns angry towards the world? Imagine how it must feel to want to fit in with the world, and the world rejects you, for that is the way right now, that this world is headed. Homosexuality is on the rise ever more, are each day, there is a new plot to corrupt the minds.

I think now about a story of a straight man who was out there looking for love, while meeting a supposedly "female" online, and hoping to have a good time. As this straight man ends up meeting with this thing, he regrets to find out that "she" is a "he", and was hiding under loads of make-up, and dressing the part, however, the man parts were still there. These are the worst kind of homosexuals, those who are so lonely, they try to corrupt the straight men, and women. For I can't leave out the fact that there is a lot of gay lesbians out there, and many try to take aim at straight women, hoping to convert them to the mental dark side. It's like a virus, and these heathen are possessed, while hoping to destroy that which is good. As that straight individual found out the worst thing possible, even while being the loneliest guy, who just may have been one that had trouble finding a date, finally finds someone to reach out to him, and it turns out to be one of those loneliest gay men, that can't find a gay lover, and so, that homosexual tries to convert this guy, hoping that lust of the flesh, and desperation would take over the capability to restrain from any form of interaction. The outcome for that homosexual, and that straight man ended up for the worst, as both of them lost their lives. The straight guy, hoping to find a female, ended up killing this homosexual, for messing with him, and that could have been the breaking point for that straight man who was seeking love, and failed time after time. That selfish homosexual, while trying to get his own, couldn't find other homosexuals alike to be with, and ended up messing with the wrong straight man, and lost his life in the process. As the straight man killed him, in the process, lost his life, while getting caught, and facing time in prison. As he now is in a worst situation, where the hopes of finding a potential wife, is gone, and so is his freedom. The damage that one can do unto another due to selfishness is disturbing to witness. It's a true shame that this straight man lost his life, knowing he should be a free man today, due to this mental illness of this so called homosexual.

It's one thing to be accepted, and even respected, but it is another thing to go so deep in trying to convert straight peoples lives. Once those with this mental illness of homosexuality, cross that line, they are now doing more evil than from the start of being gay. They tend to get people in trouble, and in worst cases, die over their doings. Just like that so called "bi-sexual", that selfishly decides to sleep with men and women, while spreading disease, and viruses, towards the straight, and that is where all of these STDs (sexual transmitted diseases) come from. It's the doing of wickedness.

Personally, I do not want to hear the voice of a homosexual. That doesn't mean I hate them and want to kill them. It is just my personal preference, and I dislike for weaker men that choose to take on this route "unfortunate trend" that is spreading around. I would never accept a homosexual into my home, nor would I ever want to keep acquaintances with them, for I know I would not be comfortable accepting what I am against, into my home, and ultimately into my life. This reminds me of times during my younger life, when I was seeking roommates. I would specifically mention those who I would want to rent to, and those who I was not comfortable with at all, and refused, while posting online in an ad. I would hear the most from homosexuals that were filled with anger, and rage, while wanting to have the opportunity to live with me. That is so disrespectful on their end, knowing I have a choice, just as they have a choice, and your household, is your own. What you decide to do, is totally up to you. As I didn't want to live with people of other beliefs, nor with homosexuals, lesbian, nor gays, it bothered them, and it was as if I should tear down my morals, and values, to accept their wickedness, and lack of shame, while having too much pride. That's like accepting crackheads into your household, or heavy drug users. No!

SCRIPTURE
Proverbs 16:5
King James Version

5 Every one that is proud in heart is an abomination to the LORD: though hand join in hand, he shall not be unpunished.

S C R I P T U R E
Proverbs 29:23
King James Version

23 A man's pride shall bring him low: but honour shall uphold the humble in spirit.

I even heard one say, "what if Black people weren't accepted, how would you feel?", and as ignorant as that sounds, it sure doesn't compare to the same issue at hand, yet, I took no offence, for I know that us Blacks (Israelites), do not need to be where we are not wanted, for that is how peace operates best., and beside that, we are still not accepted everywhere, which is fine by me. What goes against your nature, goes against your life. It's like having your enemies close to you, why? I do not want to live with my enemies, nor be close to them at all. I do not want to work with them, nor be acquainted with them period. For I know that is like having negative energy around you always. When I see that enemy, I know that it is going to be war. So, for those bitter gays that can't find love, nor find a place to live, seek out your own. It's that simple. As I took the time to find people that looked like me, on the inside, and out, over money, it benefited me more in the end. Sure, you will come across a few bad apples, but it's expected. Still, I would rather do what benefits me in the end, for it is my choices, and all the responsibility, the trials, and errors, is on me in the end, which I am comfortable to accept nonetheless. It came off even worse while having some homosexuals show up at my door, hoping to bypass my rulings. How ignorant, selfish, and foolish individuals they must be to do such a thing. They must have wanted to prove a point, but it did not work knowing I rejected them, and was big enough of a man, to not be intimidated, especially standing at over 6' tall, and a bodybuilder. Maybe they thought that they could possible have it out with me verbally, face to face, but that never happened, knowing it wouldn't end well for them in the physical form, and verbally.

It's the worst when these gays want to force themselves to be liked, and accepted by straight men, and women. It's a thin line, and that line should never be crossed. As an Israelite (Black, African American), if I am not liked, I do not go where I am not wanted. It's as simple as that. I do not hide my stripes to fit in. As I wear my fringes, with the ribbon of blue, I go where I want to go, and always wear them, even to work. If it's not welcome, I leave. Yet, these homosexuals tend to hide their gayness. They may have came out of the closet, but they are wearing mask still. They know what it entitles, as much as they know what it will result to while trying to fit in with the same friend, and even family at times. They do not want to lose nor miss out, for they fear what the result may be. But how about the other side? What about those who have morals, and values to uphold? That to me is selfish. I think about basketball, and other physical sports. A man should know who is gay surrounding them, and have the choice to play with them or not. Such with any form of spreadable sickness, such as HIV, and AIDs. For, you wouldn't be so physical with a homosexual, knowing you can catch such viruses through the blood. Imagine MMA fighting? They beat one another up, until blood of the opponent in on the other often. How would it be to have someone else blood mixed in with your own, if you are hiding in the closet, while not caring about others? The only word that best describes it, is selfish.

The attitude of these angry, lonely, and rebellious homosexuals is disturbing to witness at all levels. As we see and witness this world unfold, and become more sinful, it is now destroying the lives of many, due to the choices of certain individuals that force themselves in the room, and at the table. It is one thing to be accepted, and to come out of the closet, but to force themselves into the lives of others, and within the schools, as well as, our normal lifestyles, is not pleasing at all.

Rejection is hard on many levels, and if you cannot accept it, you are not living in truth. Without truth, there is only lies, and with lies, it is deceiving, for nothing is real. It's time to repent or face the second death which is to come, due judgment day.

CHAPTER
8

REPENT OR DIE
(IT'S YOUR CHOICE)

SCRIPTURE
Luke 13:5
King James Version

5 I tell you, Nay: but, except ye repent, ye shall all likewise perish.

A choice, is still in your faviour, for those who choose wrong, face the second death, while those who choose right, may just be saved. Yet, it is a choice, and that choice is while you are living here today. As long as you have life, you have a chance. This is a message to all the lost sheep of Israel, being, Blacks, Negros, African Americans. As long as you have life, you can change your ways. You can repent. You can turn from the wicked ways that you were once doing. But how much time do you think that you have? It's time to look at life in a new light, and it's not to go along with the program that the government has established. It's time to do things better, and follow the righteous ways that the Messiah has set forth for us to follow. You know deep down inside of you that you are not living right. No matter how much you pretend to live this lie, and cover your iniquities, you can't beat the mirror, for the mirror will certainly tell you the truth.

SCRIPTURE
1 John 1:8-9
King James Version

8 If we say that we have no sin, we deceive ourselves, and the truth is not in us.

9 If we confess our sins, he is faithful and just to forgive us our sins, and to cleanse us from all unrighteousness.

As you can read about what the power of repentance, and confessions can do. Likewise, my sin used to be fornication, until I repented of such things. For as I learn more about cleanliness, the more I learn about how much I love my body, and do not want to live with any form of sickness. I do not know your situation, and I do not know what made you become gay in the first place, but I'm guessing it is due to the lust of the flesh, and lack of options, being raised soft, or by being persuaded by another homosexual. It's due to your upbringing, and the soft way that you were raised. All that you were, and all that it may have been, doesn't need to stay the same way for ever, especially when you open your mind to the truth. Many homosexuals deny the truth. They ignore and hate it when people expose them of their evils ways, yet, they expect for people to understand, respect, and accept their ways around them, when we who know it is against nature, will never accept such people, nor ever feel comfortable surrounding them. Do not be deceived, more than you are deceiving yourselves. For before you lie to me, you must first lie to yourself.

I remember a guy that I hired for a work contract that I had set up. Not knowing he was homosexual until I met him, I, being a child of YAH (GOD), spoke my mind and addressed how foul it is for him to choose such a route. As he even said that he believe in the Most High, he in front of me chose his lifestyle over the Creator. Instead of repenting, he was comfortable, and openly selecting the route that he was then introduced to. As I was working on the task at hand, I heard him on the phone with his gay partner, and it was disgusting to hear. We never worked together after that, for I cannot have people around me behaving such ways. Never would I want to make people think that him, and I were an item. Though I do not care for what people think, I damn sure am not going to make myself feel any ways uncomfortable, and it was knowing I couldn't stand to hear a grown ass guy talking to another guy with a weak voice, behaving like high school sweat-hearts, yuk! Before you hate me, you must hate yourself, for I live in the truth, I speak the truth, and I am honest, as well as am respectful before being disrespectful to all nations of people. If you hate that, then you hate reality, it starts with you.

SCRIPTURE
1 Corinthians 6:11
King James Version

11 Know ye not that the unrighteous shall not inherit the kingdom of God? Be not deceived: neither fornicators, nor idolaters, nor adulterers, nor **effeminate**, nor abusers of themselves with mankind,

10 Nor thieves, nor covetous, nor drunkards, nor revilers, nor extortioners, shall inherit the kingdom of God.

11 And such were some of you: but ye are washed, but ye are sanctified, but ye are

justified in the name of the Lord Jesus, and by the Spirit of our God.

If you are a weak man, you will never inherit the kingdom of the Most High. One thing about all men, we are all equipped with the same tools to be husbands, fathers, and men in general. We are all capable of speaking, while using our tongues. Yes, there are men that are smarter, and stronger than you, however, it cannot take away from you being a man within yourself. We are all capable of defending ourselves, and even being capable of learning. We all can learn. The only difference between one man and another, is the mindset. When one is confident, the other is not. When one is strong, the other decides to become weak. When one is confident, the other is not due to low-self-esteem, and lack of confidence. Who is to blame? Those who find excuses, and are weak in the mind, as well as the flesh, are just weaker individuals due to not wanting to step up to the plate. If I being 6' tall, and muscle bound, step into a wilderness with a lion, and there is a 7' tall man, as well as a 5' tall man. Which man is not a man? That is a silly question, for we are all men. What we do doesn't change anything towards each of us, however, our actions can be made more than the other, for the 5' man can certainly go and face this lion, while I know for sure, I'm out of there, and the 7' man may just be more food for the lion to attack, ha ha. It's how you think. In truth, I would face that lion, for I can't run too fast, and would rather go head up, while using all my energy, but it is what it is, and it is an example. We all can get a swing a bat, but some choose to not even want to attempt the opportunity to hit that home run. And for that same reason, is why so many decide to change who they are, while living a lie. This change that needs to come, must start with you, while you drop all the excuses and weaknesses within them mind.

S C R I P T U R E
Romans 1:24-32
King James Version

24 Wherefore God also gave them up to uncleanness through the lusts of their own hearts, to dishonour their own bodies between themselves:

25 Who changed the truth of God into a lie, and worshipped and served the creature more than the Creator, who is blessed for ever. Amen.

26 For this cause God gave them up unto vile affections: for even their women did change the natural use into that which is against nature:

27 And likewise also the men, leaving the natural use of the woman, burned in their lust one toward another; men with men working that which is unseemly, and receiving in themselves that recompence of their error which was meet.

28 And even as they did not like to retain God in their knowledge, God gave them over to a reprobate mind, to do those things which are not convenient;

29 Being filled with all unrighteousness, fornication, wickedness, covetousness, maliciousness; full of envy, murder, debate, deceit, malignity; whisperers,

30 Backbiters, haters of God, despiteful, proud,

boasters, inventors of evil things, disobedient to parents,

31 Without understanding, covenantbreakers, without natural affection, implacable, unmerciful:

32Who knowing the judgment of God, that they which commit such things are worthy of death, not only do the same, but have pleasure in them that do them.

As we all know it, whether you are a believer in the Messiah, and the Most High, in prophecy, or not, you cannot deny the signs. You cannot deny that history is out there, and you cannot deny all that is to come, knowing the Scripture is unveiling everything before our faces. I look at Sodom and Gomorrha, I look at the old earth that passed away during Noah's time. This world was flooded, and as the drought has hit the seas, we can now see a life that was before our time, and they are the fossils in the ground that is the history proof. Those who choose to not repent, will fall and this time around burn in the lake of fire. You have an opportunity to repent of your sin. If you do not take heed, Noah's art will not be a place for you, but this time around it will be the lake of fire, and garnishing of teeth. There will be flames instead of floods of water.

SCRIPTURE
Jude 1:7
King James Version

7 Even as Sodom and Gomorrha, and the cities about them in like manner, giving themselves over to fornication, and going after strange flesh, are set forth for an example, suffering the vengeance of eternal fire.

SCRIPTURE
1 Timothy 1:10-11
King James Version

10 For whoremongers, for them that defile themselves with mankind, for menstealers, for liars, for perjured persons, and if there be any other thing that is contrary to sound doctrine;

11 According to the glorious gospel of the blessed God, which was committed to my trust.

As I've given you this book, and even supplied you with Scriptures from the Holy Bible, you now know right from wrong. You know to do better, and you know that the life that you live, is foul, and needs to change. Allow this following verse to help you to understand how crucial it is to choose life and death today. If you choose to ignore, that is on you, and your soul. That is on everything that you call your life.

S C R I P T U R E
Acts 3:19-26
King James Version

19 Repent ye therefore, and be converted, that your sins may be blotted out, when the times of refreshing shall come from the presence of the LORD.

20 And he shall send Jesus Christ, which before was preached unto you:

21 Whom the heaven must receive until the times of restitution of all things, which God hath spoken by the mouth of all his holy prophets since the world began.

22 For Moses truly said unto the fathers, A prophet shall the Lord your God raise up unto you of your brethren, like unto me; him shall ye hear in all things whatsoever he shall say unto you.

23 And it shall come to pass, that every soul, which will not hear that prophet, shall be destroyed from among the people.

24 Yea, and all the prophets from Samuel and those that follow after, as many as have spoken, have likewise foretold of these days.

25 Ye are the children of the prophets, and of the covenant which God made with our fathers, saying unto Abraham, And in thy seed shall all the kindreds of the earth be blessed.

26 Unto you first God, having raised up his Son Jesus, sent him to bless you, in turning away every one of you from his iniquities.

SCRIPTURE
Romans 1:32
King James Version

32 Who knowing the judgment of God, that they which commit such things are worthy of death, not only do the same, but have pleasure in them that do them.

REPENT
OR DIE!!!

THE CHOICE IS YOURS..

LIST OF SOURCES

- **The Holy Bible** (King James Version)
- **The Apocrypha** (King James Version)

- Please note that I do not own the pictures being used.

DEVRET CLARKE
Homosexuality
is a Mental Illness

DEVRET CLARKE
BEHIND THESE DOORS
YOU REALLY DON'T KNOW ANYBODY

DEVRET CLARKE
TAKE UP THY CROSS

THE NARROW PATH
WRITTEN BY:
DEVRET CLARKE

We All Go Through It,
The Journey Called
"LIFE"
WRITTEN BY:
DEVRET CLARKE

THE
RIGHTEOUS
WALK
What Happened to
Morals and Values ?
DEVRET
CLARKE

DEVRET CLARKE
THROUGH THE STORM
THE BENEFITS OF
LONGSUFFERING

YOU CAN'T WIN WITH JEALOUSY
WRITTEN BY:
DEVRET CLARKE

WHAT
HAPPENED
TO THE
MANLY
MAN
?
DEVRET CLARKE

DEVRET CLARKE
No Sympathy For The Wicked

DEVRET CLARKE
EXPOSING
THE WAYS OF THE
WICKED

WHITE
COLORED
SEGREGATION IS NECESSARY
BY: DEVRET CLARKE

WHITE
COLORED
SEGREGATION IS NECESSARY 2
EXPOSING THE ENEMY
BY: DEVRET CLARKE

Still Sleeping?
WAKE UP!
Dedicated to the
12 TRIBES of
ISRAEL
WRITTEN BY:
DEVRET
CLARKE

Still Sleeping?
WAKE UP!
PART 2
WRITTEN BY:
DEVRET CLARKE
DEDICATED TO THE 12 TRIBES OF ISRAEL

THIS
GENERATION
SIGNS OF THE END
Written By:
DEVRET
CLARKE

DEVRET
CLARKE
REAL TALK
JUST SPEAKING MY MIND

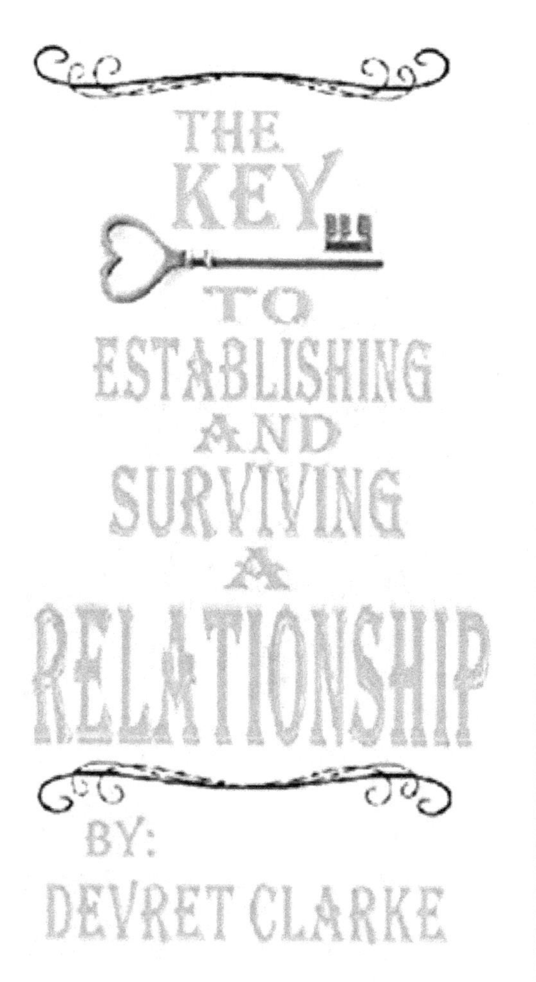
THE
KEY
TO
ESTABLISHING
AND
SURVIVING
A
RELATIONSHIP
BY:
DEVRET CLARKE

by: DEVRET CLARKE
LOVE IS NOT LOVE, UNTIL LOVE LOVES YOU...

DEVRET CLARKE
USED

DEVRET
CLARKE
BE
THE
EXAMPLE
NOT
THE
EXAMPLE

DevReT CLarKe
MIRRORS
Do you believe yourself?

DEVRET CLARKE
THE INTERNET ERROR
THE SURVIVAL OF HUMANITY

THE WAR
OF
WORDS
Written By:
Devret
Clarke

THE
TEMPORARY
VOICES INSIDE
MY HEAD
Devret Clarke
Facing:
Unwanted Telepathy, witchcraft, sorcery, & "Gang-stalking"

KNOW WHEN TO RIDE
DEVRET CLARKE

Book Author,
DEVRET CLARKE
Website - DevretClarke.ca

Like what you read?
Support the author. All blessings are appreciated.

https://www.paypal.com/donate?
hosted_button_id=TMM43TPRV2VT
N